HOW TO DEVELOP A
'NEVER GIVE UP'
ATTITUDE

HOW TO DEVELOP A
'NEVER GIVE UP'
ATTITUDE

DR. HARDIK JOSHI

Notion Press

Old No. 38, New No. 6
McNichols Road, Chetpet
Chennai - 600 031

First Published by Notion Press 2016
Copyright © Dr. Hardik Joshi 2016
All Rights Reserved.

ISBN 978-1-946390-44-8

Dedicated to

my beloved parents

and my aunt...

CONTENTS

....

Acknowledgements   *ix*

Introduction   *xi*

1. Dream   1

2. Visualisation   11

3. Affirmation   19

4. Plan   27

5. Effort   35

6. Focus   43

7. Determination   55

8. Self-motivation   67

9. Persistence   77

10. Gratitude   87

11. Celebration   99

A Real 'Never Give Up' Story   *107*

ACKNOWLEDGEMENTS

. . . .

I wish to express my heartfelt gratitude to my parents, Naresh Joshi and Mamta Joshi, for their encouragement and prayers. They have always loved me and supported my choice.

There are no words to describe my gratitude to my aunt, Maya Joshi, whose unconditional love has been my greatest strength. Special thanks to the rest of my family for providing me the strength to keep moving forward.

My sincere thanks to life coach, international speaker and entrepreneur Michelle Amod for her valuable guidance during my journey of writing this book.

I would also like to thank to the team at Notion Press for their help in publishing this book.

INTRODUCTION

....

Smooth roads never make good drivers.

Smooth seas never make good sailors.

Clear skies never make good pilots.

A problem-free life never makes a strong person

– Unknown

Dear readers,

Human beings have been facing problems and challenges ever since the time of evolution. Problems are a part of our lives. Whatever progress we have made so far is the result of man overcoming problems. But often many of us forget this truth. We become so conscious of our problems that our mind cannot think about the solution. Instead of fighting adversities, we bow in front of them.

As a result, we are forced to give up our dreams. We compromise with our lives. Instead of taking risks, we find a safety net everywhere. We lead a monotonous life, forgetting the purpose for which God sent us to Earth. We must remember that we are not here to live a stereotyped life but we are here to make a difference. We must also not forget that one cannot enjoy the sweetness of joy without tasting the bitterness of sorrow.

Finally, at the time of death, we regret not having taken risks, having missed out on opportunities, and not chasing our dreams.

Ask yourself this question, "Why is it so?"

The answer is: the absence of a 'never give up' attitude.

The attitude is a powerful weapon in the battle of life against enemies such as fear, frustration, depression and anxiety.

Everybody wants to have a 'never give up' attitude but they are often plagued with this question: is it possible to develop a 'never give up' attitude?

The answer is YES.

Then another question is this: how do we develop this attitude?

This book is their answer. This book will teach you how to develop a 'never give up' attitude.

Let us see look at these words closely.

	Letters
Never	5
Give	4
Up	2
Total:	11

The phrase 'never give up' is made up of eleven letters. Eleven qualities are required to develop this attitude. This book discusses in detail each quality.

You may also have this question in your mind.

Who will benefit from this book?

The answer is everyone who has a desire to develop this attitude. It does not matter whether he or she is a student, a jobseeker, an employee, an employer, a businessman, an athlete, a homemaker, a researcher or an artist.

To give a creative touch to the book, I have tried to compare each quality with an organ, except the last one. The last quality has been compared with neurotransmitters.

At the end of each chapter, I wrote a real life story. These people are not film stars or celebrity. These are ordinary people who became extraordinary because of their 'never give up' attitude. I hope these small stories may inspire you.

Over to you, dear readers.

– Dr. Hardik Joshi

CHAPTER 1

DREAM

'Dream' is a word made up of five letters. It has tremendous potential. Dream is the first baby step towards achieving any kind of goal or aim. Dream is like the foundation of a building. It is the base on which you work towards achieving something. As we know, the strength of a building depends on its foundation. Likewise, the likelihood of achieving your goal depends on how strong your dream is.

In this book, I am not going to discuss the dreams we have while sleeping. Because we don't have a control over ourselves when we are sleeping. So, we don't have a control over the dreams we have during sleep.

This book discusses the following:

- The dreams of our choice
- The dreams that we desperately want to make true
- The dreams for which we can even die
- Dream is an imaginary image of the future. The mere thought of it pumps our hearts and

minds with energy. This energy increases our willpower and we want to achieve our goal no matter what the conditions are.

Our dream can be:

- Buying a luxury car, a big bungalow, diamond jewellery or electronic gadgets
- Securing an admission in a good school or college
- Scoring good grades in examinations
- Getting a good job with a handsome salary
- Starting a business or expanding the current business
- Being a sportsperson and winning matches
- Being an artist like an actor, director, singer, painter, writer or speaker
- Having a good-looking life partner
- Travelling the world

These are just a few examples. Each person has a different dream.

There are more than 7.4 billion people living on this planet. But only a few people can make their dreams come true. The rest of the world either faces failure or compromises with average achievements. Why do some people fail? Have we ever thought about this? Many of us may have thought about it, but perhaps we didn't find the answer.

I too have thought about it and this is what I think are some of the reasons why some people cannot achieve their dreams.

1. Most people have not been appreciated by the others for dreaming. Maybe their family, relatives, friends, colleagues and neighbours didn't acknowledge their dreams. When a person wants to do something different from the usual, he or she does not get support that easily. Instead of supporting the person's dream, people often harass him or her. They may even use abusive words and actions. Such behaviour breaks the morale of a person and prevents him or her from pursuing the dream.

2. Some people cannot forget past failures and disappointments. It is difficult for them to overcome negative circumstances and memories and make a fresh start. They are stuck in a rut like a person sitting on a rocking chair, unable to move.

3. People do not aim for anything big. They just settle for average achievements. The fear of failure prevents them from dreaming big and high.

4. People do not have the confidence and courage to pursue their dreams. They have plenty of things going on in their mind but they cannot decide which one is right. In the end, they are satisfied with ordinary achievements and live a stereotypical life.

5. Lack of imagination and the power to pursue one's dream is another reason. Man is God's best creation. Man has a special gift that is priceless—he can convert imagination into reality. But to do so, he has to overcome distractions around him efficiently.

After reading the point above, you may have questions like 'what is the solution to the problem?' and 'how can we achieve our dream?'

Well dear friends, the solution is to eliminate the above five factors and keep in mind the following observations. By doing so, we can live the life of our choice.

1. **The dream must be original.**

   We are not talking about video or audio piracy here. By 'original', I mean our dreams should not be someone else's dream. We must have our own dreams. We must be the director of our own movie called 'life'. We must take full charge of ourselves. When we live our life fulfilling others' dreams, there may be chances of facing failures or losing interest in living life. Nothing is more important than fulfilling our own dreams.

2. **Clarity of a dream is a necessity.**

   Clarity comes when a dreamer can describe his or her dream properly. We cannot talk in general terms. We must be specific about our dreams. We may write down our dreams. This brings great mental clarity. We can also write down the emotions we feel when we are dreaming. These emotions have a magical effect on us. They help us stay motivated in every situation.

3. **Be passionate about the dream.**

   Dream and passion are like the two sides of a coin. When we are passionate about our dream, we can make it true. Passion is a powerhouse that provides us enormous amounts of energy.

This energy is necessary to kick any obstacles between us and our vision. We become so enthusiastic that we are never tired or stressed and we never complain about the so-called 'obstacles' in life. Passion brings out motivation and motivation brings satisfaction.

4. **Our dream is what we decide it to be.**

We should not forget that the dream we want to make our reality is our own decision. So, we must never ever regret it. Instead of regretting, we must put endless efforts towards achieving it. There may be one, 100 or 1000 problems in our way, but we must never stop making efforts. Effort means the end of failure. There comes a day in our life when we are victorious due to our endless efforts. We must keep in mind that we can never let go of the dream we have chosen to pursue. We must be confident about the choices we have made or want to make in future.

5. **Being proud of our talent.**

Each human being on Planet Earth is endowed with a talent. One must feel proud of that talent, which is a gift from the Almighty. Our dream must be in accordance with our talent.

What happens when the dream is not based on our talent? We may then find it difficult to achieve our dream. We must design a dream on a simple yet powerful principle: *do what you love and love what you do.* Because when we do this, we need not make excuses for the efforts to achieve it. Successful people work on this principle always.

6. Be ready to pay the price.

We must be prepared to pay the price for our dream. Paying the price is not in terms of money, but in terms of hard work.

Two ingredients are required for the fulfilment of our dream. They are:

a.   Getting out of the comfort zone

b.   Always giving the best shot

We may encounter a struggling period or a crisis-like situation during our journey. There may be chances of getting frustrated too. Frustration may lead to failure. But we don't want this to happen. It is better to die trying to fulfil a dream than be stuck with disappointments.

7. Have the right people in the team.

It is very important to have the right people around us as our team. No matter how small or big their role is, it is difficult to chase our dream without them.

Well, what does the word 'right' mean? It means people who:

• understand us and value our dream

• want to help us genuinely

• not only stay with us in the good times but also stand like a rock-solid support in the bad times

• make us realise our hidden talents and bring out our full potential

- gently point our faults and help us find solutions for them

  We can easily connect with such people logically and emotionally. We can also share our ideas and experiences with them.

  Following the above steps sincerely and genuinely will lead to success.

Creative comparison of dream:

Dream is like the heart of the body.

We all know the importance of the heart in our body. No matter how strong and good-looking the body is, if the heart is not functioning properly then we may get into trouble. If it stops working, then we lose our life.

Similarly, dream is like the heart of our life. Without a dream, it is impossible to achieve anything in our life. In other words, if we do not have a dream, our life becomes meaningless.

***

This is a story of a woman who belonged to very poor family. Her family was poor, but her dreams were not.

Maya was born in 1972 in a tribal area in Gujarat, India. Her father was a labourer and her mother was a maid. She lived in a small home that didn't have even the basic facilities. As there was no electricity at home, she had to go to her friend's house every day to study.

Maya faced a very tough time during her childhood. There were times when she did not have food to eat for four consecutive days. When her friend Ripal came to know about Maya's poor economic condition, she told Maya to come to her house every morning before school to eat something.

Maya was intelligent and good at studies. She secured the first rank in the final exam of tenth standard. She and her family were very happy but their troubles did not end here. Her parents were worried as they did not have money for Maya's higher education. Maya's dream was to become a teacher and serve society, but her financial condition was the biggest hurdle. Hesitatingly, her parents told Maya that they would not be able to pay her fees and hostel expenses anymore.

Maya was disheartened but she did not give up. She was expecting a miracle in her life and it happened due to her strong desire. When Jagdish, a rich man in the village, came to know about Maya's problem, he went to her house and assured her that he would take care of her academic expenses. Jagdish had a daughter who was clever in studies. She had died at the age of fourteen due to leukaemia. She had dreamt of becoming a teacher. After her death, Jagdish decided that he would fulfil the dream of students who were good in academics but unable to continue their studies due to their financial condition. When he heard about Maya's problem, he remembered his daughter. He met Maya and became emotionally attached to her. He saw her like his own daughter. So, he decided to help her as much as he could.

Maya was on seventh heaven when she heard this. She joined a primary teacher's certificate course.

After two years, she became a qualified teacher. To help her father financially, she started working as a tutor for primary students at home. This sharpened her teaching skills. Soon Maya got job offers to be an assistant teacher from schools in five districts. She joined the school in Vadtal in Gujarat in 1993. Thanks to her dedication and passion for teaching, she climbed up the ranks fast. She is now the principal of the school. She has taught more than 5,000 students so far.

Maya dreamt big and never gave up in life.

CHAPTER 2

. . . .

VISUALISATION

Visualisation is the most wonderful gift of God to human beings. In the previous chapter, we discussed dreams and how they form the foundation of the building of achievement. Visualisation acts like a pillar on that foundation.

Let us try to understand this in detail.

Pillar provides power and support to the building to stand straight in any kind of situation. Likewise, visualisation provides power and support to our dream. It boosts our self-confidence in usual and tough conditions too. It ensures we never collapse during the journey towards achieving our dream.

To understand the term 'visualisation' better, let us look into an example. Whenever we are hungry, we look for food. When we think of food, our brain starts producing images of various foods like apples, bananas, watermelons, grapes and oranges, traditional foods, fast food such as sandwiches, pizzas, burgers and pasta, or sweet dishes like chocolates, ice creams, cakes and pastries.

During this process, our subconscious mind gets a message and makes our inner desire strong enough to get the food we are interested in. Finally, we get the food for eating.

In the earlier days, visualisation was known as 'mental rehearsal' to achieve what we have planned for. When we do the mental rehearsal of success, it draws positivity from the universe towards us. Positivity makes us powerful and emotional. The combination of power and emotion provides both physical and emotional strength, which are the key ingredients for the 'never give up' attitude. With these strengths, we can deal with any kind of situation. They make the impossible possible. They make the toughest things the easiest ones.

Visualisation gives us the will to achieve what we want to.

You may have the following questions.

1. Is there any technique to practise visualisation?

2. Is there any scientific evidence to believe in the visualisation technique?

3. If yes, is there any proven example to show that visualisation is true?

4. Who can use this technique?

5. Is it possible to achieve anything only by visualising it?

    Following are the answers to the above questions:

1. Is there any technique to practise visualisation?

There is no hardcore technique for visualisation. But there are a few methods that will help.

a. Use of senses:

As we know, human beings are gifted with the five senses of sight, hearing, taste, touch and smell. To get effective results, we must use all the five senses together. When we do this, we create harmony with the universe. This harmony brings positivity in our life, which is very important to make our dream come true.

b. Acting out:

Try acting out the dream as a reality during visualisation. The physical movement helps stimulate the brain and makes our imagined experience more real.

c. Writing down the visualisation:

The dream, which is in the mind, becomes more powerful when we write it down with a clear description. Our memory system responds well to written (or typed) words.

d. Making a vision board:

Generally, in the initial phase of our dream, we are full of energy. But as time passes, the energy fades slowly. To solve this problem, make a vision board. It is the best reminder of our goals and what we must accomplish. To prepare a vision board for our goal, use photographs, newspaper and magazine cut-outs and other visual triggers.

e. Using props:

Using props for visualisation makes our emotion strong. For example, if we want to earn $1,00,000 then do the following things.

i.   Write it down on a currency note.

ii. Or make a cheque in your name and fill in the amount you want.

iii. Stick it on the ceiling of the bedroom or on a vision board so that you look at it when you wake up in the morning. You can also keep that currency note or cheque in your wallet or purse. Look at it whenever you are free during the day.

2. Is there any scientific evidence in the belief of visualisation technique?

Yes, scientific research supports the concept of visualisation. Studies on the brain show that visualisation of an action stimulates the same brain regions that get activated when we actually perform the action.

For example, when we visualise lifting our left hand, it stimulates the same part of the brain that gets activated when we actually lift our left hand. The reason is the brain cannot make out the difference between the actual and visualised task.

3. One example that shows visualisation is true.

Here is an example that shows how effective the visualisation technique is Dr. Denis Waitley, an American motivational speaker, writer, consultant and bestselling author, took the visualisation concept called Visual Motor Rehearsal from the Apollo space program (the third United States human spaceflight program carried out by the National Aeronautics and Space Administration, which successfully landed the first humans on the Moon from 1969 to 1972) and used it for the Olympic games from 1980 to 1990.

Wires of high-tech biofeedback machines were attached to players. Players were then instructed to run the race in their minds. The research team found that the muscles that get triggered when they run on the track were fired even when the event was visualised in their minds. The reason is, as stated earlier, the brain cannot differentiate between the visualised and real race.

What you visualise, you materialise.

4. Who can use this technique?

Everybody can use the visualisation technique. It is not specific to certain people. Actors, athletes, speakers, leaders, artists and entrepreneurs have used this technique in the past and have seen tremendous success.

5. Is it possible to achieve anything only by visualising it?

The visualisation technique has brought tremendous positive results in many people's live and made them successful. But we must remember that efforts are also necessary to make the dream come true. Practising only visualisation, without putting any efforts towards our dream, may not help us that much. A combination of genuine efforts, continuous practice and visualisation techniques can secure success for us. Visualisation is only a tool that helps us take the right action.

A strong will makes us powerful to conquer anything in this world.

Creative comparison of visualisation:

Visualisation is like the lungs of the human body.

The lungs are one of the hardest working organs in the human body. They expand and contract every three seconds (or nearly 20 times a minute) to supply oxygen to be distributed to all the tissues in the body. They also eject carbon dioxide that has been created throughout the body. First, the oxygen enters the red cells in the blood. The red blood cells then carry oxygen across the body.

Visualisation functions similar to the lungs. It provides a belief (oxygen) to our dream. Through visualisation, we send a message to the universe and the subconscious mind. This helps us convert our dream into reality.

***

This is the story of a woman who was a firm believer in the power of visualisation.

Jamila Vohra was a homemaker. She was passionate about cooking and wanted to use her talent and make it big in life someday. One day, while reading a book, she learnt about visualisation and the powerful results it produced. She was so impressed by the technique that she decided to follow it. Every day, she spent five minutes daily visualising herself as an expert cook who ran a cooking class.

One day, she was watching a cookery show on TV with her husband. During the commercial break, there was an announcement about a cooking competition. Interested people had to send in a recipe to the TV channel. People whose recipes were chosen would get a chance to participate in a cooking competition. Jamila's husband urged her to send her recipe. But Jamila thought it was a tough ask as there would be several participants from across the state. So, she refused to send her recipe to the TV channel. Moreover, it was the last day for recipes to be sent.

Two days later, when they were watching the same cookery show on TV, they discovered that the deadline for sending the recipes had been extended by a week. Jamila thought this was a sign from God to showcase her talent. She also realised that regularly performing visualisation had helped her get closer to her dream. So she sent the recipe to the TV channel. To her surprise, Jamila's recipe was selected and she was invited to participate in a cooking show.

Jamila visualised her cooking winning huge appreciation from judges and viewers. She also visualised herself as one of the finalists.

Jamila cleared various levels and reached the final, where she was declared the runner-up. She bagged a contract with the TV channel as one of the hosts of a new cookery show. Due to her regular appearance on TV and her talents at cooking, she soon became famous. Jamila also started her own cooking class. People from all over the world came to her to learn cooking.

Jamila credits the power of visualisation for transforming her dream into reality.

CHAPTER 3

....

AFFIRMATION

The word 'affirmation' comes from the Latin word 'affirmare,' which means 'to make steady, strengthen.' Affirmation makes our mind firm to achieve what we want by making us believe that it has already been achieved by us.

Today's world is full of negativity. The prevalence of negative incidents and negative personalities is higher than the positive ones. The different media such as print (newspapers, magazines), electronic (television, video) and social media highlight and discuss the negative issues more than the positive ones. Most of the times, we as human beings keep reinforcing our negative beliefs, knowingly or unknowingly.

Are you surprised by this?

Well, in our day-to-day life, we use some of the sentences below:

I can't do this.

I am not that powerful.

It is tough for me.

How foolish am I?

I am going to fail.

I am not that rich to afford this.

These are only a few examples. There are many other ways in which we continuously harm ourselves.

Now, you may wonder why I am focussing on the negative stuff.

The answer is, when we say something negative or act in a negative way, we are sending a message to our subconscious mind and to the universe. Both of them are like robots. They follow instructions without any questions and produce the results accordingly. If we think and speak negatively, it means we are affirming ourselves with the negative stuff.

If we want a positive change in our life, we must change our negative mindset and the negative environment around us. We must detach ourselves from negativity and start focussing on positivity. This is the best and only way to feel the positive power in us. This positivity is the basic requirement of affirmations.

Affirmations are result-based. By practising positive affirmations, we can achieve what we want in our life.

Many of us may have a series of questions in our minds regarding affirmation.

1. How does affirmation work?
2. Is there any specific procedure?

3. How much time does it take to get the results?

4. Is positive affirmation really helpful?

5. Are there examples of affirmations for the various aspects of life?

1. How does the affirmation work?

Positive affirmations rewire the brain by breaking the patterns of negative thoughts, dialogues and actions. Affirmations increase our strength and potential to take the necessary action to transform a thought into reality. With affirmation, we start believing that nothing is impossible.

When we practise affirmation, not only in the form of thoughts, but in action too, we develop a deep sense of confidence to convert any kind of dream into reality.

It has been scientifically proven that, along with the brain, the universe also plays an important role in affirmation. We must think before we speak. When we say 'I cannot' or 'I am not', both the universe and the subconscious mind create a favourable situation. Similarly, when we say 'I can' or 'I am', both the universe and the subconscious mind create a positive situation for us. Repeated positive statements help us focus on the dream and turn it into a reality.

2. Is there any procedure for affirmation?

There is no standard method for practising affirmation. But we must take care of the following points.

The affirmation should not be long. It must be short and clear.

a. The mind must be in a relaxed mode, free from everyday tensions such as driving in traffic or crossing a busy street.

b. Repeat an affirmation at least hundred times.

c. Sentences used for affirmation must be in the present tense and not in the future tense. For example, if you want to be rich, then the affirmation should be 'I am rich' rather than 'I will be rich' or 'I want to be rich'.

d. Avoid negative words in affirmations. If someone wants to lose weight, the affirmation should not be 'I am not fat' or 'I will lose weight'. Instead, one must say 'I am getting fitter' or 'I am getting towards the ideal weight'.

3. How much time does it take to get the result?

The objectives we want in our life may happen immediately, in a few hours, days or weeks. Sometimes it takes even a month, as it also depends on how small or big the dream is.

The main factors that contribute to the timeframe are:

a. clarity of focus

b. strength of our faith

c. depth of desire

d. the feeling we put in our words

4. Is positive affirmation really helpful?

Absolutely, but the only condition is one must have a positive mindset. Because if we repeat the positive affirmations for a few minutes or a few hundred times with a negative mindset, it nullifies the positive thoughts. Eventually, it affects our dream and the time it takes to achieve it. So, we must eliminate negative thinking.

5. Examples of affirmation in the various aspects of life:

Different people play different roles such as a student, an employee, a businessman, a sportsperson or a life partner. The affirmations differ based on the roles played.

As human beings, we are full of desires. We want a healthy body and mind, good money, good grades in the exam, a good job and a successful career.

Each desire has its own set of affirmations.

For a healthy body and mind:

I am physically and mentally fit.

My body and mind are healthy.

My body is functioning great.

If someone is ill, then the affirmations are:

I am recovering from the illness.

I am well and medication-free.

For earning money:

I am wealthy.

I am sailing on a sea of wealth.

I have $ _____ in my bank account.

For securing good grades in an exam:

My mind is powerful enough.

I easily remember what I study.

I have scored _____ % in the exam.

For a jobseeker:

I am having the perfect job.

I am having a wonderful and satisfying job.

I am more than my resume.

For a businessperson:

My business is expanding and growing smoothly.

My business is achieving the heights of success.

I am sealing all-time great business deals.

I am making huge profits in my business.

For a good relationship:

I find love in everyone.

All my relationships are loving and long-lasting.

I am in love with a wonderful person.

Creative comparison of affirmation:

Affirmation is like the veins of the human body.

The veins play a crucial role in the human body. Oxygenated blood from the heart is carried by the arteries to the various body parts. It is necessary to bring the deoxygenated blood back to the heart. Veins do this work efficiently.

Similarly, affirmation plays an essential role while chasing one's dream. Like the veins that carry the deoxygenated blood to the heart, affirmation helps us by removing negativity from us and making us positive, confident and strong enough to take necessary actions to make our dream a reality.

***

This is the story of a young man from Vadodara who was a firm believer in reciting affirmations.

Ankit was an average student. He did not like to study, but he was very curious about electrical things since childhood. From the age of twelve, he started making electrical models. After class ten, he joined the Industrial Training Institute to become an electrician. After successful completion of the course, Ankit joined an engineering company as an apprentice. During his period of work here, he started reciting an affirmation every day. He said, "I am going abroad to work for a multinational company." This worked for him.

At the age of nineteen, he got an interview call from a multinational company. The interview was in

Mumbai. He performed well in the interview and was selected. The company offered him a project in Iraq. He had to leave immediately. It was the year 2004, when United States and other countries had invaded Iraq. Ankit feared losing his life but he took up the job. He worked in Iraq for 50 days.

It was one of the toughest times of his life. Bomb explosions, continuous firing between the Iraqi army and the US army and sudden missile attacks made his stint in Iraq a risky affair. Sometimes, due to safety reasons, he and his team had to change their location too. Ankit even spent a few days in the American army camp. He was so cut off from the rest of the world and could not even calls to his family.

This is when Ankit remembered the power of affirmation again. During the tough time in Iraq, he recited affirmations.

I am mentally and physically strong.

I am confident enough to perform my duties.

I am safe.

These affirmations helped him stay focussed and gave him courage.

After coming back from the war zone, Ankit travelled to various countries including China, South Korea, Dubai and Kuwait on work. Currently, he is working as an operations head in a mining company in Zambia, Africa.

Ankit gives credit to the power of affirmation that changed his ordinary life into an extraordinary one.

CHAPTER 4

. . . .

PLAN

Definition: Prepare a **L**ayout to take **A**ctions that are **N**ecessary.

After deciding the dream, visualising and affirming it on a daily basis, the next step is to plan.

Plan is the sail that moves the dream boat in the right direction, so that the boat reaches the destination within the stipulated timeframe set by us.

The importance of planning:

a. No matter how intelligent, strong, and positive we are, if we do not have a plan to achieve our dream, we may face a delay in achieving our dream. Sometimes, we may even fail to achieve our dream.

b. No matter how small or big the dream is, with proper planning we can make it happen.

c. No matter how smooth or rough, easy or tough the road to our dream is, we can always ride without applying the brakes.

d. No matter how many twists and turns come in our journey, we can always overcome them.

With proper planning:

- a student can get good grades in an exam.

- a jobseeker can get a good job by avoiding mistakes.

- an entrepreneur who wants to start a business or has just started a business can overcome the hurdles on his or her way.

- a businessman can get maximum profits by putting appropriate efforts in the right direction.

- a working woman can balance her life at both home and the workplace.

- an athlete or an artist can perform well.

After reading this, you may have the following questions:

1. Why should we plan?
2. How do we plan?

We should plan to enjoy some of the following benefits:

- right direction
- increased efficiency
- reduced risks and failures
- achievement of objectives
- good control of the self
- motivation
- right decision-making
- creativity and innovation

In an organisation, planning provides proper coordination between the employees of various departments and helps the organisation run smoothly.

Now, let us tackle the second question. How do we plan?

At first, it seems a difficult question to answer. But once we start thinking seriously about it, we realise we can do it. We must take a diary and a pen (or nowadays we can plan on the mobile phone, tablet or laptop) and start planning.

Once we plan our day, week or month, we start working towards it. When we find that things are not going according to our plan, we start complaining about it and blame others or the situation. This is absolutely wrong. We must realise that planning is not an arbitrary decision. Proper planning is necessary to achieve our desire.

What is 'proper' planning?

Generally, there are three types of planning on the basis of how big the dream is and how much time it takes to achieve it.

1. Short-term (generally three to four days or a week maximum)
2. Medium-term (one or two months)
3. Long-term (a year or more)

According to the approximate time required, we must decide the type of planning. One must consider the following points while planning.

a. Keeping a record:

Keeping a record of the tasks we do helps maintain focus on what to do and what not to do. We must keep a diary. Nowadays, plenty of smart apps are available on the mobile phone to make a plan. There are no specific rules, but a record typically has the following parameters:

- A to-do list
- Problems faced during the execution of the plan
- Solutions to the problems faced
- Research
- Achieved milestones

b. Being clear and specific about work:

If we are not clear and specific about the work we want to do, the chances of failure are higher. It leads to loss of energy and mental stability. Whenever we plan, we must list our priorities and allot enough time for all tasks.

c. Writing the plan clearly:

Most of us think about planning only in the mind. It is not wrong to think about the plan, but do not stop with thinking alone. When we write down the plan, it registers in our mind. We can also include the schedule, the milestones and the results we want to achieve.

d. Fixing measurable milestones:

Fixing small but measurable milestones for a dream maintains the excitement as we move towards the results. In the initial days, we are very excited and enthusiastic about our dream. But as time passes, due to unplanned obstacles and other reasons, we may feel low and down. In such situations, milestones give us the opportunity to celebrate our accomplishments. It brings inner happiness and pours infinite energy for the next part of the plan.

e. Setting the timeframes:

Generally, when we have a dream to achieve, our main focus is on the final destination. We tell ourselves that by this time, for instance a couple of weeks or months, we will achieve this or that. Well, this is not bad at all. Along with this, it is very important to set the timeframes for every single objective or task. Working without a short-term timeline may lead to serious issues. Some tasks may get delayed or unfinished. Whatever be the objective and action plan, we must set appropriate timeframes for every step.

f. Marking objectives when done:

Marking objectives as and when they are done gives satisfaction and brings joy. These two feelings are very important for both individuals and teams. It reduces stress and instils confidence in what we have achieved during the journey of making our dream come true.

g. Revising the plan if necessary:

As we have discussed earlier, during the journey of converting our dream into reality, there may arise unimaginable and unwanted situations and other roadblocks. Well, that is not a big deal as this happens with everyone, whether he or she is a beginner or an expert. But what is the main difference between an ordinary person and an achiever? In difficult situations, an ordinary person gives up on his or her dream while an achiever never gives up.

If things are not going according to our plan, we must just sit with a calm mind and revise the plan. We must always remember that revision is better than regret. Moving forward with a focussed mind will turn our dream into reality.

Creative comparison of plan:

A plan is similar to the ribs of the human body.

Ribs are the flat, thin, curved and long bones that form the ribcage. The ribs provide protection to the two vital organs—the heart and the lungs. There are three main functions of the ribs.

1. The heart supplies blood with the support of the ribs. Without a ribcage, it is very difficult for the heart to supply blood to the rest of the body.

2. Breathing is possible due to the ribs. The lungs can expand and contract with the support of the ribcage.

3. Ribs are one of the few bones that continue to make red marrow (and thus blood cells) in adults.

A plan, like the ribs, is crucial to the dream. A good plan protects the dream.

The three main benefits of executing the plan well are:

1. We have a clear path to follow.
2. We come to know of the probable hurdles. Thus, a plan helps us reduce the risk of failure.
3. Plan provides encouragement to us. In other words, a well-designed plan makes our dream a reality.

***

This is a story of a man who believed that planning and execution played an important role in success.

Harman Patel was born in a family of eight members in the state of Gujarat. His father, Tulsi Patel, was a school teacher. Harman was very attached to his father and greatly inspired by him too. His father taught him the importance of having a good vision and a strong commitment to fulfil it.

Harman joined Bachelor of Chemistry after standard twelve. After graduation, he pursued a post-graduate diploma in sugar technology in Kanpur. Then he got a job in a sugar factory as a manufacturing chemist. After a couple of years, he realised that working in a sugar factory was not his ambition. He quit the job and decided to pursue an MBA in Ahmedabad. After post-graduation, he joined one of the leading pharmaceutical companies as a product manager. His incredible potential won him the management's confidence and he was promoted as the business head.

During his interaction with the young employees, Harman realised the need for training in soft skills and personality development, which schools, colleges and universities did not provide. Harman made up his mind to start an institute that would work for youth development. But it was not possible at that time due to his family responsibilities. After retiring as the vice-president of a pharmaceutical company, Harman decided to start a training centre.

Harman prepared a plan. This involved buying a place to set up the institute, meeting engineers to develop the infrastructure of the institute, hiring faculties, preparing the institute's website and marketing the institute among potential students.

Harman successfully executed his plan and started his training centre Yuvalay on July 6, 2014. Initially, students were given training free of cost. He tied up with universities to train students in various personality development programmes. He and his team went to the villages for the betterment of students there. They trained more than 5,000 students across 300 programmes in the first two years.

At Yuvalay, Harman set up a library and a unit for student counselling.

Harman is now 63. His ambition is to reach out to as many students as possible across the various cities and villages of Gujarat.

Harman credits his success to impeccable planning and execution. He still trains students for free.

CHAPTER 5

....

EFFORT

Effort means the work done by the mind and the body to do or produce something.

Effort is an attempt to do something.

We read in the previous chapter that having a dream, visualising it and affirming it every day and making a plan are essential to achieving our goal. Otherwise, everything becomes meaningless. Once we have decided our dream's plan of action, we need to put in the requisite efforts and utilise every opportunity that comes our way.

We human beings are full of desires and are passionate about something or the other. For example, some are passionate about music, some want to be an actor, while others are keen to become a writer, businessman or scholar. Some want to earn a handsome salary. But only a few hundred or, at the most, a few thousand people are able to make their dream come true.

Why does the rest of the world fail to achieve its dream? What is a big difference between the few successful people and the others who are not so successful? The answer to the above questions is 'lack of efforts'.

Why do people fail to put in the necessary effort? Following are some of the reasons:

1. In our society, people give more importance to success but they do not see the efforts a person puts in to be successful.

2. Today, everybody wants to be successful but they are not ready to put in the required efforts. People want to be successful with minimum efforts or through shortcuts.

3. Success today is measured in terms of money, power, degree etc. But efforts are not given weightage.

Being passionate about something or having a dream is a good quality, but it is not sufficient to convert the dream into reality. For that, we must put in genuine efforts. The word 'genuine' means with all our heart, mind, soul and body.

At the beginning of the dream, our efforts are higher as we are very enthusiastic. But as time passes, the intensity of our efforts reduces. This is the basic difference between the ordinary and the successful people. There are very few people who put in real efforts without excuses. In other words, excuse leads to suicide, while effort leads to achievement of the dream.

It is ironic that in our society people want to be successful but they do not want to put in the necessary efforts for it. People always appreciate the achievements than the efforts put in to achieve them.

Youngsters get the wrong message when we give importance to achievements alone.

We want to be a diamond, but we are not ready to put ourselves under the scanner and go through the processes of forming, cutting and shaping. As a result, we are satisfied with an average life.

Now, you may have the following questions:

1. What happens if we do not put in efforts?
2. How much effort should one put in?
3. How do we know whether our efforts are sufficient or not?
4. Why are endless efforts required?
5. Why should we appreciate efforts over achievements?

1. What happens if we do not put in efforts?

We must remember that when we do not give our best, we may have to eventually sacrifice our dream. Giving our 100 per cent in whatever we do is the best and only option. It boosts our self-confidence and motivation. These two are necessary weapons to move forward even for the smallest battle.

A simple but powerful reminder: when we do not give importance to our efforts, we are wasting our time and energy.

2. How much effort one should put in?

Effort is one of the hardest proven factors of life. Effort is not easily measurable. Our results cannot accurately estimate how much efforts we put in, but putting efforts will always lead to better results. It may seem difficult in the beginning, but it is worthwhile at hindsight.

Different people need to put in different amount of efforts for the same task. We must never compare ourselves with others. List out the probable tasks and divide them into various categories such as easy, moderate and tough. By doing this, we have a rough idea about the requirement of efforts.

3. **How do we know whether the efforts we have put in are sufficient or not?**

In order to answer this question, we have to ask ourselves another question: am I doing everything I can to transform my dream into reality? If the answer is 'yes', we are putting in efforts as per the requirements; if not, then we are lacking in our efforts. We are the best judges of ourselves than any other person in the world. We cannot lie to ourselves.

4. **Why are endless efforts required?**

Endless efforts are the key to opening the lock to success. Efforts make us mature. In the journey towards making our dream a reality, sometimes situations may not be in our favour. We may encounter failures. But we must remember that we are born fighters. We cannot let our dreams end up in a disaster. Whenever we are in a difficult situation or our efforts do not bring us the desired results, we must pause and analyse the situation quietly. We need to find out what mistakes we did, design a new plan and get into action.

5. Why should we appreciate efforts over achievements?

As we have discussed in the start, we always appreciate achievements in every field of life, whether it is academics, career, job, business, sports or the arts. Of course, it is good to appreciate and celebrate these achievements. But sometimes it sends a negative message to people, especially the youth, if we appreciate only the achievements and not the efforts put in by the achiever. We convince ourselves that only achievements are important and start focussing on them. If we refer to the history of achievers across all fields, one thing that is common to all of them is 'effort'. Relentless effort is one of the biggest reasons for their achievements.

When we appreciate efforts, we boost a person positively. This encouragement eventually turns efforts into achievements. The person will not take any shortcuts to success.

Given below are some affirmations that we must tell ourselves.

- *I can do this (to self).*
- *We can do this (to the people who work in the team).*
- *I know you can do this (to another person making the effort).*
- *With more efforts and trials, I will definitely make my dream a reality (to self).*
- *With more efforts and trials, we will definitely make our dream a reality (to the people who work in the team).*

- *With more efforts and trials you will definitely make your dream a reality (to another person making the effort).*

- *It is okay if things didn't work out perfectly, but I am on the right track. Let's see what I can do to make things work out even better next time (to self).*

- *It is okay if things didn't work out perfectly, but we are on the right track. Let's see what we can do to make things work better the next time (to the people who work in the team).*

- *It is okay if things didn't go perfectly, but you are on the right track. Let's see what you can do to make it work even better next time (to the person making an effort).*

Creative comparison of effort:

Efforts are similar to the spinal cord of human beings.

A spinal cord connects the brain and the body. The body and brain can communicate with each other due to the spinal cord. It is a bridge between the brain and the body. The two important functions of the spinal cord are:

a. It connects the peripheral nervous system to the brain.

b. It coordinates simple but essential reflexes that do not go through the brain. For example, the spinal cord ends a signal not to touch an object that is hot.

40

Similarly, efforts connect our dream with reality. Endless efforts are necessary to realise our dream. Every time we put in genuine efforts, we get close to achieving what we want.

Effort means end of failure.

***

This is a story of a man who always put in his best efforts in life.

Naresh Kumar was born in a lower middle class family. He was good in studies, but he failed in class twelve due to the bad company of friends. But Naresh didn't let this deter him. He joined a course at the Industrial Training Institute.

Naresh often remembered his teacher's words about efforts.

"Effort paves the way to success. Nothing worth having is ever achieved without effort. One must keep putting in efforts even when there seems to be no hope at all."

These words were imprinted in Naresh's mind forever. At the Industrial Training Institute, he put in his best efforts. As a result, he became an expert in his field.

After completing his course, Naresh got a job as a machine operator in an engineering company. Due to his curiosity for learning, he learnt to operate all the instruments in his department. He worked sixteen hours a day to save money for his sister's wedding. He was dedicated to his job.

One day, due to a small mistake, Naresh's senior manager insulted him in front of his staff. The manager said, "You are an idiot. You don't know anything about work. Nobody will hire you even at the price of salt. You will not do anything worthwhile in your life."

Naresh was shocked by this insult. He decided to prove his manager wrong. The next day, he saw an advertisement for the post of a supervisor instructor from the employment department of Gujarat. He applied for the job. At the interview, he performed well and bagged the job easily. Naresh and his family were very happy.

The next day, Naresh went to his senior manager, showed him his offer letter and said, "Thank you for insulting me."

Due to his sincere efforts in the new job, Naresh was promoted as a foreman instructor. Later in his life, he took to training others in the field.

Naresh has been training students for the last 32 years. His students have done well and secured jobs in multinational companies.

Naresh believes that everything happens for a reason. His senior manager's insult was the turning point in his life.

Naresh's life is a good example of the 'never give up' attitude and the importance of sustained efforts, despite failures.

. . . .

CHAPTER 6

FOCUS

Definition: Focus is a significant and essential part of our attention or interest.

In other words, focus is the ability to integrate our attention and energy on a particular task until it gets done.

Focus is a must-have quality for any dreamer whether he or she is a student, a scientist, a jobseeker, an employee, an entrepreneur, a businessman, an athlete or an artist.

Focus transforms us from being a beginner to an achiever.

Whether a dream is small or big, easy or tough, it requires focus. No matter how strong, motivated, enthusiastic and self-disciplined we are, we cannot make our dream a reality if we are not focussed. Without focus, a dream remains a dream.

At the initial stages of our dream, we have the best intentions and a clear-cut plan. But when we start working on our dream, we lose momentum due to many reasons. This hampers our desired progress and affects us negatively, resulting in loss of self-confidence and drive. Eventually, it results in a failure.

There may be many reasons for this failure, including lacking of resources, family problems or luck. Above all, the prime factor is lack of focus. If we are genuinely focussed on the task, we can accomplish it.

According to research, we as human beings can get distracted every three minutes. We must remember that our focus determines our reality.

Let us consider a couple of examples. There are two persons: A and B. Both A and B have a different mindset.

A wakes up with a sad mood in the morning. This sadness brings negativity in him. He focusses on the negativity throughout the day.

B wakes up in the morning thinking it is a pleasant day. This thinking brings positivity and makes his day full of positive events. In this case, B focusses on positivity throughout the day.

Let us consider another example.

While working, A's attention starts jumping from one task to another. It leads to an unproductive day as he cannot complete any of his tasks properly.

On the other hand, B focusses on a single task and works on it whole-heartedly. He completes the task with satisfaction and this results in a highly productive day.

These may seem simple and unimportant. But these are real instances. Most of us, either knowingly or unknowingly, behave like person A in our daily lives. Very few people behave like person B; these people are highly successful in their lives.

You may the following question:

Even though we put in full efforts, why do we still end up with failures?

The reason is it is difficult to think properly without focus.

Poor thinking leads to:

- poor observation
- bad memory
- poor logical and reasoning quality
- lack of a problem-solving approach
- lack of decision-making power

Lack of focus

⇩

Distraction

⇩

Lapse in concentration

⇩

Waste of time and energy

⇩

Decreased effectiveness in work

⇩

Poor quality work

⇩

Deadline missing and unfinished tasks

Another question that arises is:

What are the reasons that affect our focus and are there any ways to avoid them?

In today's world, there are plenty of things that can distract us and shift our focus from our task. This ultimately hampers our dream. But we can learn to avoid these distractions and retain our focus. We must put in genuine efforts to remain focussed.

Here is how we can remain focussed:

1. **Kicking out the garbage from the mind:**

    Our thinking directly affects our focus. So, we must try to clear the mind. It is like how we clean our bikes and cars. We take bath daily to clean our body, but we do not take care of our mind and hence the mind becomes cluttered.

    A cluttered mind always faces difficulties and cannot focus well. In simple words, when we work in such a state, we fail to give our 100 per cent to any task.

    What is a cluttered mind?

    A mind full of unimportant thoughts, worries, anxieties, fears, questions and doubts is a cluttered mind.

    To have a healthy clutter-free mind, we must dump negative emotions and thoughts. Here are some steps to have a clutter-free mind:

    - **Meditation:** A few minutes of quiet meditation clears the mind and improves focus.

    - **Taking a break from routine:** We get bored doing the same activities on a daily basis. Our mind gets an opportunity to think differently when we do different activities such as going on a tour, trekking or setting up a campfire.

    - **Talking with a friend, relative or coach:** The intensity of negative thoughts decreases when we talk to our friends. In addition to this, we also get suggestions from the people who care for us.

- **Avoiding past regrets and future worries:** Many of us worry about the future or dwell in the past. This will not lead us towards our dream. Living in the present is the best way to increase our focus.

- **Writing a journal:** Writing a journal makes us conscious about our negative emotions. Taking a blank page and writing down everything that comes to our mind helps channelise our thoughts, which eventually empties our mind.

2. Multitasking and ways to avoid it:

In today's times, many of us have become expert multitaskers that we have forgotten how to do one task at a time. Multitasking may help us sometimes, but not all the time. The chances of making mistakes are more when we do more than one task at a time.

We think that we can reduce time and energy by multitasking. People feeling proud doing this. But in reality, this is not true. We should not multitask all the time. The reason is our mind is not wired in that manner.

Let us take an example to understand this concept better.

Consider person **A** who is a multitasker. At the workplace, he (or she) works on three different tasks: He is preparing his list of tasks to finish, he is checking his email on his laptop and he is talking to a client on the phone.

Now let us put ourselves in this situation and imagine doing three tasks at a time. Will that be easy to do? There may be chances of making a mistake in any or all of the three tasks. We may not remember the important conversation we had with our client, we may miss checking an important email or we may forget to finish the key tasks of the day.

How can a person focus on a single task in the presence of several distractions?

There are crucial times in our life when we need to focus exclusively on a single task. For instance, during extremely important conversations, taking major decisions in a big project, during an examination or while performing extraordinary activities in a sports event.

Now the question is how do we avoid multitasking?

Given below are ways to avoid multitasking; they help us improve focus.

i.   **Doing one task at a time:** Even though we may have the urge to multitask, we must try to focus on a single task. It will take us lesser time to finish the task and boost our confidence. We can save our energy too.

ii. **Finishing one task first, then starting on another:** Instead of doing many tasks at a time, it is better to end one task and then start on the other. This will energise us to take on the next assignment.

iii. **Cleaning the workplace:** We must clear clutter from the workspace. A clean desk leads to better focus.

iv **Decreasing the disturbances:** Disturbance is the biggest enemy of focussing on a task. We must try to reduce, if possible eliminate, disturbances such as notifications of text, email and mobile calls. Closing unnecessary windows on the laptop, especially the ones related to social media, and closing the door to the office or the room one is working in also helps decrease disturbance.

v. **Assigning time to tasks:** Assigning time to the various tasks will clear our mind from confusion. It also helps us decide which task is of prime importance and which one is the least important.

3. **Being the master of technology and not its slave:**

We live in a digital world where there are plenty of electronic gadgets such as smartphones, tablets, laptops and computers. Constant beeps, pings, text messages, emails, vibration alerts, caller tunes, notifications from social media updates and games are big distractions today. Many surveys reveal that these gadgets greatly affect a human being's work and productivity.

We can avoid the excessive use of gadgets during work in the following ways:

1. Placing the devices on silent mode: We can stay more focussed this way.

2. Closing the windows of email and social media: This way we do not waste time on unnecessary notifications.

3. Setting logical time limits: Instead of prohibiting ourselves from gadgets, games and social media, it is better to set a time limit for using gadgets, websites and applications. This way, our concentration on our work increases and we also do not get bored.

Creative comparison of focus:

Focus is like the bones of a human body.

Bones are dynamic organs of the human body. They are responsible for the structure and shape of the body. They constantly change shape and structure to adapt to the daily forces placed upon them, thus protecting the internal organs from injury. Bones are essential for our daily existence too as they are capable of storing minerals and energy. They also play an important role in the production of red blood cells.

Like bones, focus is very crucial for our dream. Focus helps us maintain concentration in both the good and difficult times. It protects us from negative people and negative situations and helps us develop a fighting spirit. With proper focus, we can change the plan according to the situation. Hence, we save time and energy.

***

This is a story of a young man who exemplifies the power of focus.

Sagar lived in a small town of Gujarat. He came from a humble middle class family.

Sagar joined the commerce stream after class ten. His dream was to become a chartered accountant (CA). After class twelve, he migrated to Ahmedabad for higher studies. He joined the Bachelor of Commerce programme (B. Com) and also started preparing for the Common Proficiency Test (CPT), an entrance exam to join the CA programme. He studied for six to eight hours a day and successfully cleared CPT during the first year of B. Com. During the second year of B. Com, Sagar cleared the Integrated Professional Competence Course.

In the third year of B. Com, Sagar got a job offer from the Railway Mail Service department. But he refused the central government job as he was so focussed on fulfilling his dream of being a CA. He successfully completed B. Com in 2014. He then started doing M. Com and CA articleship simultaneously. He appeared for the CA final exam in November 2015 and cleared it successfully.

To remain focussed, Sagar took the following steps.

1. He prepared a plan for each stage of his study of CA and tried his best to stick to it.

2. He spent most of his time in the library.

3. He eliminated distractions like social media, internet and video games on the mobile phone.

4. He did not even meet his family on festivals.

5. He joined a group of people who were on the same mission as him.

Sagar gives credit to his family and friends who stood by him during the tough time. He also attributes his success to his laser-like focus. He finally became a chartered accountant at the age of just 21.

·················

CHAPTER 7

DETERMINATION

Determination is a powerful emotion necessary to transform a dream into reality. In other words, it is a concrete intention to reach a desired dream or goal.

Plenty of obstacles may arise while chasing our dream. They are in the form of uncertain situations, the mistakes we commit, the naysayers and the critical people around us. Determination is a strong will that can never be broken by anything or anyone while chasing our dream. There may be some people who achieve success through sheer luck but determination gets success for most people.

Determination is an amalgamation of several kinds of knowledge, skills, beliefs and talents that facilitate us to engage in our work with self-confidence.

Without determination, it is very difficult to maintain the pace to move forward. The difference between a winner and a loser, a leader and a follower is determination.

Determination is one of the most valuable qualities that every successful person has. A student who wants to gain knowledge, a researcher who is working on a tough project, a businessman who is keen to expand her business, an athlete who wants to better his game or an artist who wants to do better rely a great deal on determination.

The extent of our success depends on how determined we are. The things that seemed unbelievable or impossible to achieve earlier, like the mission to reach other planets, bullet trains and aeroplanes to reduce travel time, hi-tech devices and weapons, and world records in sports have been achieved because of determination.

1. What are the signs that show a person is not determined?

2. How does lack of determination lead to disappointment?

3. What are the ways to test determination?

4. What are the ways to be determined?

5. Are there examples of determination?

1. What are the signs that show a person is not determined?

We know whether a person is determined or not by observing the following.

- **Lack of will power:** When we are not willing to go after our dream, we start making excuses than putting in efforts. We are scared to take the necessary risks to fulfil our dream.

- **Lack of self-belief:** When we do not believe in ourselves, we do not trust our decision-making ability. This leads to dependency on others. Most of the times, people cannot understand our dream and eventually this leads to disaster.

- **Lack of self-discipline:** When we are not disciplined, we cannot give our 100 per cent efforts. This affects our planning as we cannot meet the assigned deadlines. This is one of the top-most reasons for failure.

- **Lack of flexible nature:** Being flexible and adapting to the situation is very important. We cannot be rigid all the time, especially during uncertain situations. If we are not flexible, there is higher probability of failure than success.

2. How does lack of determination lead to disappointment?

When we are on a journey, we must aspire to materialise our dream. We may face unexpected hurdles on our journey; when we lack determination, we allow these hurdles to stagnate us and we do not move forward.

The following graph gives us a clear indication of how one can spiral downhill due to lack of determination:

Obstacles

Lack of self-confidence

Decrease in optimism

Lack of focus and efforts

Development of negative attitude

Failure

We must be both physically and mentally tough to nurture determination. Toughness helps us understand that the key to success is failure. When we accept this, we will feel fulfilled instead of disappointed.

3. What are the ways to test determination?

There are two ways by which we can test our determination.

a. Determination during hard times: When the circumstances are not in our favour, we feel helpless and are ready to give up. But if we are determined to achieve our dream, we will never give up.

b. Determination is seen in the conscious decision to go with the easiest alternative in a particular situation.

4. What are the ways to be determined?

Determination is about our willingness to do whatever it takes to achieve our dream. Given below are a few ways in which we can build our determination.

1. Increasing willpower:

- Good food: We must always eat a diet that is rich in proteins and carbohydrates. This helps our brain take important decisions.

- Predicting the roadblocks: Predicting the roadblocks prepares us to fight against adverse situations. It reduces our fear and increases our willpower.

- Deciding the reward before starting the task: Choosing rewards (chocolates, watching our favourite TV programme or playing a video game) increases our willpower to finish the task within the deadline.

- Quality sleep: Adequate sleep for seven to eight hours provides us the necessary rest and reduces the body's need for glucose, which is important for the brain too. Rest rejuvenates both the body and the brain, and ultimately increases our willpower.

- Meditation and exercise: A combination of meditation and exercise acts as the powerhouse of willpower. Meditation gives us peace of mind and increases our clarity and focus. Exercise increases the strength of our body and mind and keeps us in good shape, physically and mentally.

2. Increasing self-belief:

- Belief in the self is the first step towards building a determined mind. No one will believe in us till we start believing in ourselves.

- Setting small objectives and accomplishing them: When we focus only on the big tasks, there may be chances of failure. And this may discourage us. Setting small objectives and achieving them gives us a good feeling. By practising this habit, we feel better and eventually build self-belief.

- Avoid comparing ourselves with others: It is human nature to compare ourselves with friends, relatives and colleagues. When we compare ourselves with others, it results in an inferiority complex. We start thinking that we are not really good at anything. This harms our self-belief. Avoiding comparisons will not only increase our self-belief but will also build strong relationships with others.

- Appreciating the achievements: We have the habit of looking at what remains to be achieved rather than appreciating the achievements so far on the journey towards our dream. We must develop the habit of identifying and acknowledging our achievements. This enhances our strengths and builds a positive self-image, which ultimately results in self-belief.

- Dealing with the negative inner voice: We must find out if the voice within us is ours or is the opinion of others. If we do not do this, we may feel that the inner voice is ours and not realise that it is others'.

- We can recharge ourselves by watching motivational videos and movies, listening to inspirational songs and speeches.

3. Developing discipline:

- Developing a strategy: Discipline is a learned skill, not a natural characteristic. In other words, we can develop self-discipline. All we need is practice. Many of us do not know this truth. As change is difficult in the initial stage, developing discipline takes time. But it is worth the effort. Discipline cannot be achieved overnight. We need a strategy to develop it. Whether we want to develop a good habit or eliminate a bad one, we need to develop a plan so that we can acquire discipline.

- Tolerating emotional uneasiness: Often we try to run away from negative emotions like stress, dullness, frustration, sadness and loneliness. But this is not the right way to deal with these emotions. Trying to deal with emotional uneasiness makes us strong and helps us increase our discipline.

- Eliminating the temptation: We believe that we are strong enough to stand against temptations but it is not always possible for us to do so, as we are constantly surrounded by things that ignite our temptation. Try making access to temptations difficult. This can increase our discipline. For example, if social networking sites and apps are our weaknesses, then we must stop using the internet during work.

- Discipline is a continuous process. If we stop working on it, we will slowly begin to lose it. We have to keep working on our discipline.

4. Increasing flexibility:

- Successful people are flexible in nature. We know that it is not sensible to use the same approach for every situation. Even though we know this fact, we do not act according to it. We become rigid both physically and mentally during hard times. This causes pain to us. We must accept that some storms are inevitable in life and we need to take a detour to avoid them.

- Adjusting and adapting: Unexpected and expected events can happen anytime. But in most of the cases, we cannot handle them properly. This creates disturbances. We must possess tolerance for uncertainties as this helps us remain stable, both mentally and physically.

- Improving self-confidence: The major reason for avoiding change is fear. Fear makes us worried about coping with change. Boosting our self-confidence can moderate our fear of change. One of the most effective ways to boost self-confidence is mental rehearsal.

- Self-stretching: People who do the things in a routine manner have a lot of trouble coping with change. Not stretching ourselves can create rigidity in us. Trying to do the same task in various ways increases flexibility in our nature.

- Practising yoga: Yoga helps us increase both physical and mental flexibility. It helps us maintain a feeling of being centred. Subsequently, we find our mental, spiritual and emotional balance. Yoga helps reduce our stress, tension, fear and anxiety.

Creative comparison of determination:

Determination is like the muscles of the body.

Muscles provide strength to the body and help us in movement. Muscles store energy in the form of glycogen. They give us balance and posture. The heart is made up of muscles and we know how important the heart is. We develop muscles and make them stronger by exercising regularly.

Similarly, determination provides the strength to our dream. Determination strengthens our belief in achieving our dream even in difficult conditions. Just like we can develop muscles through exercises, we can develop determination by practising various techniques.

***

This is a story of two friends who became businessmen thanks to their sheer determination.

Shiv and Siddharth were from the city of Vadodara in Gujarat, India. They met each other during the first year of college. Though they had different personalities, they became good friends. Shiv was interested in marketing and Siddharth was interested in sales. After college, they decided not to take up a job and instead start their own business.

During the mid-nineties, the computer industry was very popular. So, Shiv and Siddharth decided to start a computer hardware and software business. The biggest challenge for them was both of them did not have too much knowledge of computers.

Nobody believed in them at that time. Their parents said to them, "Business is not in our blood. Do not take unnecessary risks. Chances of failure are higher than success." Friends warned them about their lack of knowledge regarding the computer industry. Relatives advised them to forget the idea of starting business.

The atmosphere around them was highly negative. But they were determined to start their business. They ignored the negative noise around them and kept motivating each other. Because of their determination, they rented a small place and set up their shop. Shiv took care of marketing, while Siddharth concentrated on sales. They faced several financial constraints during the initial years. Despite facing a loss in the first year, they did not lose hope or courage. They continued their business and never gave up.

As time passed, their hard work brought rewards. They have now three large showrooms and a service station and they employ more than 25 people. Theirs is one of the leading service providers in the city.

Shiv and Siddharth are self-made millionaires. They proved that if someone is determined enough, nothing one can stop him or her from converting the dream into reality.

CHAPTER 8

SELF-MOTIVATION

Self-motivation is a person's ability to fulfil a dream or goal without getting affected by interruptions in the form of people and circumstances.

Whenever we have a dream to achieve, we must visualise it, recite affirmations and prepare a workable plan. We must also put in efforts with focus and determination. But sometimes, due to odd circumstances, we cannot transform our dream into reality. Due to this, the excitement to accomplish a dream, scoring good grades, getting a good job or being promoted, starting a business or expanding a business by securing new deals, setting a new record, winning a medal as an athlete, giving the best performance in a show or writing a good article or a book, vanishes suddenly.

Sometimes, we cannot even explain our feelings. We are desperate to get our energy and momentum back. But we don't have to worry too much about it. This happens to every successful person. We must remember that every successful person was a beginner once. One of the differences between a successful and an unsuccessful person is a weapon called motivation.

Successful people beat tough situations through self-motivation.

Why is self-motivation required?

Self-motivation is not only required when we cannot achieve our dream, but it is also required when we are in the right direction.

Sometimes, even when we are in the right direction, we struggle to continue the march as we are disturbed by various factors such as:

- negative thoughts
- regrets about the past and anxiety about the future
- doubts
- depression
- criticism
- loss of loved ones

We cannot make genuine efforts if we remain stagnant in the same condition. Motivation is the positive energy that keeps us focussed despite any of the above issues. Without motivation, we may find ourselves engaged in unimportant and unrelated tasks. Due to this, our dream remains unfulfilled. Motivation provides us the momentum to keep trying until we convert our dream into a reality.

How does lack of self-motivation affect us?

When things do not happen according to our expectations, we experience shortage of energy and enthusiasm. This makes us mentally and emotionally drained. Not only this, we also lose courage and hope and this eventually leads to failure.

Lack of self-motivation

Shortage of energy and enthusiasm

Mentally and emotionally drained

Loss of courage and hope

Failure

What are the factors that decrease our motivation and how can we improve self-motivation by overcoming these factors?

It is possible to regain lost motivation. In fact, it is necessary to do so. Many people believe that it is not possible or it is very difficult to develop self-motivation. But we can develop self-motivation through a few easy steps. We must be enthusiastic and stay committed to every step of the way till we achieve our worthwhile dream.

Following are the factors that affect self-motivation and ways to overcome/deal with them:

1. **Fear:** We must remember that fear leads to failure. Fear is one of the prime reasons why many people do not achieve their dreams.

Fear freezes us from marching towards our destination. Sometimes a person cannot even start his or her journey due to fear. Fear makes us anxious and depressed too.

How do we overcome fear?

Dealing with what makes us scared is the best way to eliminate fear. When we start doing what we are afraid to do, we find our fear vanishing gradually. We must ask ourselves questions such as:

1. Why do I fear this?

2. Is the fear real or imaginary?

We can overcome fear by trying to find the answers to the above questions. Remember that imaginary fears will go away easily. Real fears need analysis and a plan to overcome them.

2. **Procrastination:** The second most common reason for lack of self-motivation is procrastination.

    There are two types of tasks:

    a. important but less pleasurable tasks

    b. less important but pleasurable tasks

    Procrastination pulls us back from accomplishing the tasks that are less pleasurable but important. We busy ourselves in pleasurable tasks that are not important. We postpone type A tasks and perform the type B tasks immediately. This creates feelings of guilt, self-doubt and depression.

How do we overcome procrastination?

1. We must make a list of the pleasurable and less pleasurable tasks.

2. We must identify the reasons for not doing the less pleasurable tasks immediately.

3. We must plunge into the less pleasurable task straightaway. We may find that it is not as bad as we thought it was.

4. We must reward ourselves after completing each less pleasurable task.

3. **Criticism:** When we are chasing our dream, we will be criticised for our dream or approach. It seems difficult to accept criticism. But we must handle the criticism. In fact, we can use it in two ways:

   a. We can use criticism in a positive way and improve ourselves.

   b. Or we can let criticism affect us negatively and lower our self-esteem. This leads to stress, anger or aggression.

   There are two types of criticism:

   Destructive criticism: There are negative people around us who criticise us always. The reason why they do this is either they do not know what we are doing or they do not want to see us successful. They use abusive words, negative comments and negative actions to solve their purpose.

How do we overcome destructive criticism?

   Negative criticism is meaningless and irrational. We must never give importance to it. Doing so decreases our self-belief and enthusiasm towards our dream. We lose self-control and get angry. Eventually, we lose our momentum, focus and determination towards our dream.

The best way to avoid such criticism is to keep as much distance as possible from such people. We must not let their words and actions disturb us.

Constructive criticism: There are some people like teachers, coaches, friends, loved ones and family members who want to see us successful. So, they may criticise us for the mistakes we do. We may find this annoying. But they are the ones who cannot see us in pain due to difficulties or failures. Their criticism shows us where we are going wrong and how we can improve.

Constructive criticism should be considered as useful advice that can help us improve ourselves. It is not meant to put us down. We must accept constructive criticism though it is a little painful to our ego. If we do not understand why someone is criticising us, we must ask them directly. We can also ask them for suggestions to correct our mistakes. This will create positivity in our relationships, which ultimately makes us positive. This positivity is a key ingredient of the self-motivation recipe.

4. **Lack of positivity around the self:** We must have positive and inspiring people around us. When we do not have such people around us or if we are surrounded by negative people and situations, our motivation dips and we may get caught in a web of negative emotions.

How do we overcome negativity and create positivity around us?

Finding inspiring people: We must always have inspiring and positive people around us. We need to find them. We must make a list of inspirational people like friends, relatives or even a celebrity and be in touch with them regularly. We must show their importance in our lives by expressing our gratitude to them on various occasions.

Making a list of quotable quotes: Remember inspiring people's golden words. Write them down. Whenever we feel low, we can recollect or read these words. This will act as a morale booster.

Doing activities that boost our energy: Activities like helping a needy person and hobbies like dancing, singing and exercising increase our positive energy. We must do such activities for an hour every day. This will generate positive energy in us. We can then use this energy to make our dream come true.

Creative comparison of self-motivation:

Self-motivation is like the liver in the body.

The liver is one of the most vital organs in the human body. It stores fat soluble vitamins (A, D, K, E) and glycogen. It stores energy in form of sugar and makes it available whenever the body needs it. Liver detoxifies the blood by eliminating harmful substances such as alcohol and drugs.

Similarly, self-motivation is a vital quality to possess while chasing our dream. It is the powerhouse of positive energy and momentum to march ahead in easy as well as difficult times. Self-motivation detoxifies us by eliminating negativity from within and the surroundings.

Without a healthy liver, it is very difficult for a person to live a healthy life. Without self-motivation, it is very difficult to make our dreams come true.

***

This is a story of a man who believed in the power of self-motivation.

Manoj belonged to a middle-class family but his dreams were high and mighty. He loved to read books, especially motivational books. These books taught him to dream big and never settle for average achievements. Inspired by the books, Manoj decided that he would not lead an ordinary life.

When he was in college, Manoj had very few clothes. He did not even own a bicycle and borrowed his brother-in-law's bicycle to go to college. But he dreamt of owning a car in the future. In 1988, he pursued an undergraduate degree in commerce. After college, he joined a pharmaceutical company as an office assistant. He was never afraid of challenges. He believed that every challenge led to proportional growth in life. He was always ready to take on as many responsibilities as he could. Due to this nature, the management promoted him to a trainee executive in a short period of time.

With hard work, dedication and enthusiasm, Manoj climbed up the ladder of success. He never set boundaries around himself. He was always willing to learn new things in his field. His passion in work and his loyalty towards his company won the trust of the management and he was promoted as the general manager of the commercial department.

To maintain the optimum level of motivation during the good and bad times, Manoj used the following techniques:

1. He prepared a vision board including photos of all the goals, aims and dreams he desired to accomplish and placed it in his room. It helped him retain his goal in mind.

2. He watched inspirational and motivational movies.

3. He listened to motivational music.

4. He was in the company of positive and uplifting people.

5. He gave himself rewards for every milestone achieved.

Manoj's dreams do not end here. His dream is to become the director of the company.

Manoj gives credit to self-motivation for his success.

CHAPTER 9

PERSISTENCE

Persistence is the ability to be dedicated and committed to one's purpose, regardless of the setbacks along the way. In other words, it is the ability to stick with something until it gets done.

Every single living object on Planet Earth, whether it is a human being, an animal, a bird, a plant or a tree, requires persistence.

There are tough times in everybody's lives.

For example:

- A student finds it difficult to concentrate on studies due to low scores and distractions.
- A graduate cannot crack the interview and fails to get the desired job.
- An employee does not get a promotion or an increment.
- A businessman fails to get good deals.
- A homemaker fails to manage the house.
- An artist or an athlete cannot perform well despite good preparation.

If we do not have the quality named persistence, it is very difficult to keep going during the tough times. Persistence prepares us to fight against adversities. It makes us both physically and mentally strong. Persistence does not let our vision get blurred. With persistence, we can stay focussed and determined. It is a skill we must develop to have a balanced and happy life and achieve what we want.

A few questions may arise in our mind.

1. Why is persistence important when we are chasing our dream?
2. How does lack of persistence lead to failure?
3. What are the factors that affect the persistence and how do we overcome them?

1. Why is persistence important when we are chasing our dream?

Persistence provides power to the person to chase his or her dream. There are some days when we feel an emptiness in our lives. There are no positive results to our efforts. There is also no positive feedback or encouragement from others. This is very common and it happens to every single person. No matter how motivated we are, if we do not have persistence, it is impossible to continue on our journey. We may lose motivation momentarily when we do not get the desired results but we must never lose the persistence to pursue our dream.

2. How does lack of persistence lead to failure?

Persistence makes us powerful. The chances of failure increase if we are not persistent. Without persistence, we become impatient. We lose self-control and this leads to negative emotions like fear, anxiety and frustration. It also costs our willpower. We do not give enough time for self-development and our dream, ultimately leading to failure.

Lack of persistence

⇓

Impatience

⇓

Loss of self-control

⇓

Fear, anxiety, frustration

⇓

Decrease in willpower

⇓

Less time for self-development and dream

Failure

3. What are the factors affecting persistence and how do we overcome them?

No matter how passionate, talented, intelligent, knowledgeable, influential or strong we are, there is always the chance of us giving up our dream if we are not persistent enough. There are some factors that impact our persistence. We must be very careful as we cannot afford the suicide of our dream.

Following is a list of negative qualities that affect our persistence and various ways to overcome them successfully.

1. **Impatience:** One of the biggest enemies of persistence is impatience. Today, people are highly impatient all the time. People want everything to happen with clockwork precision. And they also want everything to happen instantly.

   How do we overcome impatience?

   We often forget the basic truth that all things are not the same and different things take different times to grow. We must inculcate the art of patience. We must remember that instant schemes often fail.

   Following are some ways to overcome impatience:

   a. **Tracking the triggers:** Tracking the triggers that make us impatient is the first step towards getting rid of the problem. When we know and analyse the situations that make us impatient, we can develop a defence system against them.

   b. **Practising patience:** This is a simple but powerful way to test and develop our patience. We must sit quietly at least for five minutes or more without doing anything.

Initially, we may think this is not a big deal. But as the minutes pass by, we realise that it is very difficult to remain still and patient. When we practise patience on a daily basis, we can raise our patience levels.

c. **Utilising our free time properly:** When things are not working properly and we do not have any other alternative than waiting, we must utilise that time by doing something we like the most. We can also think about the most pleasurable moments of our life. By doing so, the feeling that we are wasting time vanishes.

2. **Eagerness to quit:** The eagerness to quit is an enemy of persistence. While chasing a dream, many of us have a strong urge to quit. There are various reasons for this: fear of failure, things not working according to our plan and unexpected situations. We become worried and feel guilty about the temporary defeats we are facing. Sadly, many of us quit when success is just around the corner. If only we had persisted a bit more, we could have attained success.

How do we overcome the urge to quit?

Whenever we are faced with a tough situation in life, we must pause and think about the situation.

We must ask ourselves the following questions:

a. What is wrong with the situation?

b. Am I acting emotionally instead of thinking things through?

c. How much energy and time have I invested in this?

d.   Did I start chasing my dream just to quit in the middle?

e.   Would my life be better if I gave up on my dream?

We must try to answer the above questions sincerely. The answers help us understand the real value of our dream.

3. **Habit of blaming others and situations:** This is a very common quality possessed by many of us. When things are not going according to our plan or if we have a bad day at the workplace or at home, we start blaming the situation or the person around us. By doing so, we may feel temporary relaxation but it increases our misery. When the blame-game becomes a habit, we entrust our life's steering wheel to other people and situations. We do not find out what is wrong and why it went wrong. We just leave the situation or problem and blame others, instead of putting in the necessary efforts to solve the issue. Some people start blaming themselves needlessly. This may lead to low self-esteem, a negative personality and loss of self-belief, and these are poisonous for the dream.

How do we overcome this?

We must understand that blaming others, the situation or the self is not the solution to the problem. In fact, the blame-game makes us mere losers.

a. **Taking responsibility:** Instead of blaming the situation, others or the self, we must take responsibility for the mistakes we commit. We must remember that it is natural to make mistakes as a human being. When we take responsibility for our mistakes and try to find the reason for things going wrong, we can solve the issue easily.

b. **Forgiveness:** When we stop blaming and start forgiving, there is stability and peace of mind. Forgiveness helps us let go of the past and focus on the present.

c. **Flexible approach to the cause:** One of the reasons for blaming others is possessing a rigid mindset. When we try to see an issue from several angles, we can explain the truth better. Eventually, we realise that the role of others in the problem is negligible. A flexible approach to the cause is one of the key ways to developing persistence.

4. **Laziness:** One of the most dangerous enemies of human being is laziness. It locks our mind and body from taking necessary actions to move towards our goal. Laziness also stops us from developing ourselves by learning new skills and techniques, which are important for persistence. Laziness brings negativity in our attitude. We dwell on negative things, instead of doing something new or different. Instead of being productive, we spend our time doing unimportant and unnecessary tasks.

How do we overcome laziness?

a.   **Counting the benefits:** When we feel lazy about our dream, we must count the benefits of accomplishing our tasks and achieving our dream. This helps us eliminate negative thinking, obstacles and hurdles. Focussing on the advantages motivates us to take the necessary action.

b.   **Doing the simple tasks first:** Laziness is an inner resistance to continue performing existing tasks or starting a new task. This can be overcome by doing the simple tasks first. When we do the simple tasks successfully, we feel charged and confident to take on the next task.

c.   **Thinking about the importance:** We are concerned about the benefits, damage and loss when we do certain tasks. We don't want to suffer a loss or a damage. This is due to our lazy attitude. If we realise the importance of being active, we can push ourselves to take the necessary actions.

Creative comparison of persistence:

Persistence is like the kidneys of the body.

Kidneys have critical functions in the human body such as:

- filtering toxins, excess salts and urea
- balancing the water level
- regulation of blood pressure, red blood cells and acid

If the kidneys do not function properly, then we may land in trouble. If they stop working, we may even lose our life.

Similarly, persistence helps us stay positive by eliminating negativity from us during the difficult times. Our dream expires in the absence of persistence.

***

This is a story of a man who is a living example of persistence.

Jayesh was an employee of a medium-scale engineering company. He worked there for more than fifteen years. He migrated to the US with his family in 2003 and his time of struggle began.

Jayesh did not have a good command of the English language. The first thing he did was learn English so that he could work well in the new environment. He did not have enough money at that time. So, he stayed in his relative's home in Los Angeles for four months in the beginning. He found a job in a motel for a low salary. He soon quit the job and moved to Alabama. There he found a job in a motel again.

Jayesh's situation was akin to that of a man in the middle of the sea. He was desperate to save his life. He had some missteps and took a few steps backwards but he did not get discouraged. He remembered his father's words: "It seems impossible to pass the times of difficulties but remember that the fruits of persistence are sweet. Never lose sight of your ultimate desire. Always keep yourself open to possibilities and paths. The more you persevere, the more you succeed in your life."

Jayesh moved to New Jersey and tried to find a job there. He found a good opportunity in Virginia. He again moved from New Jersey to Virginia. He worked for seven months here. Due to financial constraints, he had to change six jobs across three states in the first year. But his father's words became his strength.

During this period, Jayesh dreamt about running his own grocery store. In the year 2005, Jayesh bought his first grocery store in Virginia with his hard-earned money. But he did not stop at this. He worked harder than before. As he was new to the business, he did commit a few mistakes. But his persistence met with success. He soon bought four stores and gas stations.

Today, Jayesh is among the highest taxpayers of Virginia. He is a self-made millionaire who exemplifies the power of persistence during hard times.

....

CHAPTER 10

GRATITUDE

Definition: Gratitude is the quality of being thankful and showing appreciation for an act of kindness.

Gratitude is one of the greatest gifts of God to human beings. And it is absolutely free. One does not have to pay anything to anyone for being grateful. The one who is always grateful for everything in life is blessed with more occasions to be grateful for.

There are times when we feel depressed, stressed, frustrated, anxious and scared when we are on a mission to make our dream a reality. Our mindset turns negative from positive. We feel stuck in a situation and our dream seems impossible to achieve.

We cannot always blame the situation or people for the hard times. Sometimes we are also responsible. We always complain about the situation or the people, sometimes even God, forgetting about our positive possessions. We are stuck with negative thoughts like 'the situation is not good', 'nothing is going according to my wish' and 'why me?' We expect good things to happen to us even though we nurture negative thinking. How is it possible?

If we practise gratitude regularly, we can fight against negative emotions. The more grateful we are for our experiences, which make us stronger, the more worthwhile our journey will seem.

Gratitude is a miracle. It turns the impossible things into possibilities.

We express gratitude for various reasons. We remember good memories and are thankful for them. We count the blessings of the present and be thankful for them. We can also be hopeful and optimistic for good things to happen in the future.

Without gratitude, it is difficult to maintain high spirits in life. Gratitude is the key ingredient to increase the quality of our lives.

For example, with gratitude:

- A student can score well.
- A teacher or professor works hard to improve the quality of education.
- An employee or businessman works hard and his or her productivity increases.
- An athlete or an artist gives his or her best performance every time.
- A homemaker can effectively manage the home.

Now, one may have questions like:

1. How can expression of gratitude help us achieve success?
2. What are the ways to express gratitude?
3. What are the benefits of expressing gratitude?

1. How can expression of gratitude help us achieve success in our dream?

When we express gratitude towards others, a situation or God himself, it brings positivity in us and in our relationships with others. It also makes us empowered and optimistic in any situation of life. Instead of focussing on unproductive actions, we take productive actions. These actions bring positive results and eventually we succeed in our dream and all other aspects of life.

Expression of gratitude towards others, a situation or God

Brings positivity in us and our relationships

Makes us empowered and optimistic

Leads us to take productive actions by eliminating unproductive ones

Results in positive results and finally success

2. What are the benefits of expressing gratitude?

Various studies say that expressing gratitude brings in social, physical and psychological benefits.

Given below are the benefits of expressing gratitude.

a. **Gratitude makes us happy:** Gratitude is one of the most trustworthy methods to increase happiness and satisfaction in life. It also boosts feelings of pleasure, optimism, enthusiasm, joy and other positive emotions.

b. **Gratitude makes the relationship stronger:** Gratitude strengthens our relationships. Our relationship with our life partner, family members, society and God improves significantly. It helps us see the role played by others in our life. It helps us appreciate what others did for us and are doing.

c. **Gratitude makes us healthy:** Gratitude makes our immune system stronger, reduces symptoms of illnesses, lowers blood pressure and reduces negative emotions like anxiety, stress, fear and worry. When we practise gratitude on a daily basis, our brain generates feel-good chemicals. It also encourages us to do more exercises.

d. **Gratitude helps us sleep better:** We become worry-free when we count our blessings instead of counting our problems. This makes us peaceful and we can sleep better at night. Quality sleep increases our focus and concentration on our passion.

e. **Gratitude increases our tolerance:** Nowadays, there is an alarming rise in the intolerance level of people due to many reasons. People are not ready to forgive each other's mistakes, both at the professional and family levels. When we practise gratitude, we can forgive easily, as we do not depend on people or situations.

f. **Gratitude makes us kind:** When we practise gratitude on a daily basis, we become kind towards others. We help people and try to understand their problems.

g. **Gratitude develops our personality and career:** Gratitude makes us less self-centred and less materialistic. It decreases our feelings of jealousy, anger and frustration. Practising gratitude increases our self-esteem and makes us more spiritual. These factors are important to develop a good career.

3. What are the ways to express gratitude?

There are various ways to express gratitude to the people around us, to God and the self. These methods are very simple and effective. By practising them, one can feel positivity in the self and see the change around.

a. **Thank-you notes:** A thank-you note is the simplest and most effective way to convey how important a person is in our lives. Writing a thank-you note for the help he or she rendered during difficult times or for staying with us during tough times makes us stronger and strengthens our relationship with that person.

b. **Gratitude journal:** Writing a gratitude journal brings satisfaction. There are various ways to write a journal.

   i.   We must write down three positive things that happened during the day, no matter how big or small it was. We must also describe how we felt during those times.

Sr. no.	Positive incident	Feelings about the incident
1		
2		
3		

   ii. We can meet a family member, relative, friend or colleague and convey our gratitude to him or her. If a meeting is not possible, then we can call or text the person. We must then note it down in the journal. Also, note down the person's response to your expression of gratitude.

Sr. no.	Name of the person	Reasons for expressing gratitude	Response of the person
1.			
2.			
3.			

c. **Small cards:** We can also make small cards and write small thoughtful messages of gratitude like these:

I am thankful for_____

I am glad_____

Stick these cards on things we use frequently like the mirror, TV, office desk or refrigerator.

Complete the sentences whenever you come across these cards.

For example, you could say:

I am thankful for having a superb day.

I am glad to meet my friends.

I am thankful to God for such a beautiful life.

I am glad I secured good scores in the exams.

I am glad I secured the business deal.

I am thankful for doing a great job.

I am glad I delivered the best performance till date.

When we practise this exercise on a daily basis, we help our mind focus on the positive aspects of life.

d. **Prayers:** God is with us in every phase of life. When we are in trouble, we must express our gratitude to God for teaching the important lessons of life instead of cursing him. In good times, we must say 'thank you' to God for giving us the chance to make our life beautiful. Reciting prayers and chanting mantras are the best way to appreciate His presence in our life.

We can use sentences like:

I am thankful to God for helping me in every phase of my life.

I am grateful to God for making my life successful.

e. **Focussing on purpose:** When someone gifts us something or helps us, instead of thinking about how big or small the gift or help is, look at the thought and purpose behind it. When we focus on the purpose, it is easy to be grateful. It seems difficult to do this initially, but continuous practice makes us capable of being grateful for even small favours and gifts.

f. **Daily gratitude meeting:** Decide the time to be grateful for every single day. For example:

- when we wake up or before we go to sleep

- before lunch or dinner

- during break time in school, college or office

During this predetermined time, we must think about our good possessions and express our gratitude for them. By doing this, we feel good about ourselves, our life and others too. This brings us positivity and peace.

Creative comparison of gratitude:

Gratitude is like the brain of the human body.

The brain connects with the spinal cord and forms the central nervous system, which enables a conscious communication with our body and the automatic functioning of essential organs. The more we use the brain, the more efficiently it works. Not only this, the brain connects with each system in the body. It helps us perform essential operations such as breathing, maintaining blood pressure and releasing hormones. If it does not work properly, the human body may suffer severe problems.

Similarly, gratitude is like the brain of a dream. The more we express gratitude, the more chances we get to express it. It also helps us to connect with the self, other people and God. If we do not express gratitude for our possessions, we may miss the opportunity to convey to others and God as to how important their role is in our lives.

***

This is a story of a young man who was passionate about helping students carve a better future for themselves.

Deep was born in a middle class family. His father was a clerk. Her mother was a homemaker and she taught him the lessons of gratitude. She always told him, "Always be grateful no matter how good or bad the situation is. The more we express gratitude, the happier we are."

Deep wanted to go abroad for higher studies. So, he joined an IELTS coaching centre after class twelve.

At the coaching centre, Deep observed an absence of specific methods for preparation.

Deep quit the programme and joined the British Library in Ahmedabad. He then embarked upon a process of self-learning. There he became friends with many corporate employees. Though he was from a Gujarati medium school, Deep scored a band score of seven in the English speaking and listening tests in his first attempt. Everything was going according to his plan. But his travel agent did a big mistake during the visa procedure due to which Deep could not go abroad even though he was qualified. Instead of being disappointed, he expressed his sincere gratitude to God. Gratitude released all his disappointment. Then he joined the Bachelor of Commerce programme.

As Deep understood the basics of IELTS well, he decided to train students for the test. His intention was to reduce the difficulties of students as much as he could. In his first batch, he had six students. Due to financial constraints, Deep could not set up a dedicated coaching centre. So, he coached students in their homes. He never compromised on the quality of training as making money was not his priority. His hard work paid off as the trained students started referring other students to him.

In the year 2011, Deep started a training centre in his home town in Gandhinagar, Gujarat. It was called the Milestone Academy. He took classes for seventeen hours a day from 7 a.m. to midnight, due to which he developed a swollen vocal cord. The doctor advised him not to speak for a month but Deep did not quit coaching. He continued coaching students in sign language. The students performed better than before; many of them secured more than seven bands.

Deep was very committed to his students. Despite a raid by the Income Tax Department and the Directorate General of Central Excise in his home, he continued to train students.

Today, Milestone Academy produces the highest number of top scorers in the IELTS exam in the city of Gandhinagar.

Visit the following link to get an insight into Deep's success story and understand the importance of nurturing gratitude for what we have in our lives.

https://www.facebook.com/pateldeep69/

....

CHAPTER 11

CELEBRATION

Though celebration is an important quality of life, it is one of the most underestimated and underutilised qualities in our mission to make our dream a reality. You may wonder why I am emphasising so much on celebration. This chapter will explain why.

Many of us find celebration a highly challenging task but it is not.

Some of the common reasons we give to deny ourselves the joy of celebrating:

I will celebrate once I finish the task completely.

I will not celebrate till I achieve my dream completely.

Things are not that perfect that I have to celebrate.

I have a long list of problems. How can I celebrate?

I do not have sufficient time and money to celebrate.

What will others think about my celebration?

We also wait for occasions such as birthdays, anniversaries and festivals to celebrate.

How does lack of celebration lead to failure?

When we work continuously without celebration, we get into a rut. If we do not celebrate the little joys and successes in our lives, we do not enjoy our work. When we do not enjoy work, there are higher chances of getting stuck or making errors. This will create self-doubt, guilt and procrastination and reduce self-respect, self-love and self-acceptance. We stop trying genuinely to achieve our dream and eventually this leads to failure in life.

Continuous work without celebration

Lack of enjoyment

Chances of getting stuck and errors in difficult situations

Self-doubt

Procrastination and guilt

Decrease in self-respect, self-love and self-acceptance

Lack of genuine efforts towards our dream, ultimately leading to failure

How does celebration help us seize success?

We forget traditional festivals and important occasions in today's hectic life. We are so busy earning money, name and fame that we forget to celebrate the small successful moments while chasing the dream. But it is important to pause and celebrate every little win.

Celebration helps us in various ways.

1. **Celebration helps us stay in the present:** A majority of us have the tendency to regret the past and worry about the future. We often think about the missed chances in the past and the challenges of the future. In simple words, we forget the basic rules of living in the present. This is one of the biggest reasons for disturbances in our life. We forget the little achievements and progress we make every day. Instead of forgetting these tiny steps, we must celebrate them regularly. We must not judge our achievements as big or small. Celebration helps us stay in the present. It makes us aware of our power to chase what we want.

2. **Celebration increases self-love, self-acceptance and self-respect:** Two crucial qualities required to chase any dream are self-love and self-acceptance. But we often judge ourselves in a negative light. We give love and respect to others. We also accept their mistakes. But we are too harsh on our small failures. Despite making commendable progress every day, we become critical of our actions. We dwell on the negative issues alone. When we do not give importance to every little success

in the journey of life, our love towards the self decreases. We cannot accept failures with ease. This leads to a decrease in self-respect too.

When we start celebrating the little accomplishments, our love towards the self increases gradually. We can accept not only the small failures but the big ones too, as our respect towards the self increases. In other words, a combination of self-love, self-acceptance and self-respect helps us overcome any difficulty and make our dream a reality.

3. **Celebration amplifies positivity:** When we do not celebrate success, there is a rise in self-doubt. This self-doubt brings negativity in our attitude and causes troubles. If we want to complete the big tasks and accomplish big things in life, we must start celebrating every little achievement of ours. Celebration helps us develop a positive mindset. We start considering things positively; even the worst situations are viewed under a positive lens. We cannot be easily trapped in a negative mindset. Celebration acts like a magnifying glass. It helps us see the positive things over the negative ones clearly.

4. **Celebration helps us in achieving future dreams:** One may wonder why I am giving so much importance to celebration. You may also wonder how celebration helps us in our future dreams.

When we celebrate the small and big accomplishments towards our dream, we create good and positive memories, either knowingly or unknowingly. Good memories have a positive impact on us. They help us when we chase another dream in the future. Whenever we are faced with a difficulty, we must remember the celebratory moments of the previous dream and make ourselves positive. Past celebration boosts us to move forward and take the necessary steps towards achieving the current dream.

What are the ways to celebrate?

There are many ways to celebrate. But we need to celebrate in such a way that it helps us make beautiful memories, which we can recollect in the future.

1. **Celebrating with the people we love**: People like friends, family members, relatives and colleagues value our achievements. They know how much hard work we have put in and how much we have struggled. Celebrating with such people helps us create happy memories and our bonds with them become stronger. So, the next time we face any difficulty, we must remember our loved ones who remind us about our capability to deal with any situation. When they tell us "don't you remember the last celebration? I need a celebration party for this task too", tremendous confidence pours into us.

2. **An achievement diary:** It is very important to focus on the small achievements on a daily basis. For this, we can maintain an achievement diary.

   We must analyse the day before going to bed and write down three to five achievements, both big and small. After doing this, we must focus on every achievement and describe how it made us happy and how strongly it impacted us.

Sr. no.	Achievements	Feelings about the achievement
1.		
2.		
3.		

While chasing a dream, we must break it into smaller milestones. When we reach the milestone, we must note down 'yes' or 'no' against it and our feelings about it.

Small milestones	Achievement status (Yes/No)	Feelings about the achievement
M1. _____		
M2. _____		
M3. _____		

Doing this exercise on a daily basis will help us develop an attitude of celebration.

3. **Taking a break:** Another way to celebrate is taking a break and doing something different from our routine. Take a vacation from work. Do the activities that interest you. For example,

skiing, diving, climbing or active sports. When we do such activities, we refresh ourselves and also make life-long memories. These memories boost us during tough times.

4. **Acknowledging people:** Sometimes we forget to acknowledge the people who played an important role in our success. We do this knowingly or unknowingly. When we acknowledge others for our success, it brings peace, joy and inner happiness.

5. **Treating ourselves:** Often when we celebrate our success, we do it with other people. But sometimes it is necessary to celebrate alone. Whenever we achieve a target, small or big, we must do our favourite activities, like watch a movie or a game, eat our favourite food or play our favourite game.

6. **Ways to celebrate in the workplace:**
   - Picnics with colleagues
   - Appreciating and acknowledging each other's contributions
   - Awards such as 'Employee of the Month' and 'Employee of the Quarter'
   - Gifts and incentives to employees to motivate them to do their best

Creative comparison of celebration:

Celebration is like dopamine and serotonin.

Dopamine and serotonin are two of the most important hormones in our body. Dopamine motivates us to take action towards our goals and desires. It also gives us pleasure. Serotonin is known as the happiness hormone. It helps us stay away from loneliness and depression by regulating our mood and making us happy.

Similarly, celebration is like dopamine and serotonin. Celebration gives us pleasure. It motivates us towards our dreams, cravings and requirements. It makes us excited for the present as well as the future. It also protects us during the difficult times.

A REAL 'NEVER GIVE UP' STORY

Dear readers, this is a real story of a young man. After reading the story, I hope you say, "This man is a real example of the 'never give up' attitude."

He was born in a small city of Gujarat in India. When he was just seven months old, he was afflicted by a serious illness. The doctors could not find the reason for it. He spent 17 days with tubes in his nose. He could also not eat through his mouth. The doctors told his parents that it was very difficult for them to treat the baby and he may die if the situation continued. The doctors and the baby's family gave up hope. But the baby did not give up on his life. He fought really hard against the illness and survived.

The child became healthy as time passed. He started going to school. He was very good at studies and always secured good marks. At the age of 12, he found something unusual happening with him. He started suffering from negative thoughts continuously. But, at that time, he did not give much importance to this problem. Little did he know that it would cost him a lot in future.

At the age of 17, once again he started suffering from the problem. This gradually led him to depression. A student, who was so intelligent and always secured good grades, was able to secure only 50 per cent in his final exam. With a broken heart, he joined the Bachelor of Science (B. Sc) course. In the first year, he secured a first class and in the second year a distinction. He worked hard and was one of the toppers in the university.

Everything was looking good but he was still suffering from the problem. In the third year, the problem became so severe that he was forced to tell his parents about it. His father took him to the family doctor. The doctor asked the boy a few questions and prescribed some medicines. He also told his father, "If the problem continues, then you have to take your son to the psychiatrist."

The boy did not feel well even after taking the medicines. So, his father took him to the psychiatrist. The psychiatrist diagnosed the problem as obsessive compulsive disorder (OCD) with depression. He gave the boy some medicines but there was no counselling. The boy took the medicines for a month and then stopped taking them as he was feeling well. He secured a first class in the final year of B.Sc. He then pursued a master's degree (M. Sc) in chemistry.

Stopping the medicines was his biggest mistake. In the first year of M.Sc., the problem began to appear again. It slowly increased in intensity. The young man could not deal with it and told his father that he could not live life anymore with this illness. Everyone in the family was worried about him.

His father took him to another psychiatrist, whom the boy considered the first angel of his life. The doctor explained to the young man, "What happens to people having such a disease?" The boy started crying. The doctor told him in one sentence, "Only an extraordinary person suffers from OCD." It was a magical sentence for the young man. His health improved dramatically due to the psychiatrist's treatment. The young man successfully completed his M. Sc. with a first class. Then he took up a job in a reputed company for five months. But his goal was to pursue a career in research. So, he quit the job and took up a Ph.D. programme.

The problem surfaced again. The young man took the help of another psychiatrist. He was worried, but he did not lose hope. He hoped that one day a miracle would happen in his life. On June 30, 2012, he met another doctor, whom he considered his second angel sent by God. This doctor changed his life completely. The psychiatrist told him that he had to first know about the disease well. He also said, "You need not just medicines but counselling as well. That is very important." The doctor taught him various techniques that improved his health unbelievably. The young man completed his Ph. D in July 2013.

He then began his career as an assistant professor of chemistry, teaching students of graduate and post-graduate programmes. But he was continuously thinking about doing something to spread awareness about mental health and help people suffering from mental illness around the world. He started spreading awareness through a blog and delivering lectures. After serving as an assistant professor for more than two years, he left the job and started working as a full-time motivational speaker, trainer and counsellor. He is the founder and CEO of Thumbs Up Foundation. Currently, more than 5,000 people from 75 countries are connected with the foundation.

Who is this man? Any guesses?

He is none other than the author of this book. Dr. Hardik Joshi.

Thank you.

To send me an email

Email: drhardiknjoshi@gmail.com

To connect on Facebook

Facebook ID : hardikjsh96@yahoo.com

**To read article on various subjects,
please visit my blog**

Blog: www.thumbsupmovement.wordpress.com

Contact no +91 9898517661